This Book Belongs To:

RELAXING COLORING TIPS

1. FIND A QUIET SPACE, SET THE MOOD OR YOU CAN TURN ON SOME MEDITATION MUSIC.

2. PREPARE A FULL SET OF COLORING TOOLS.

3. CHOOSE THE PICTURE YOU LIKE AND START COLORING.

4. DON'T WORRY ABOUT GETTING EVERYTHING PERFECT, JUST RELAX AND ENJOY COLORING. YOU'LL FIND IT IS A GREAT WAY TO REDUCE STRESS AND IMPROVE YOUR MOOD.

5. FINALLY, WISH YOU HAVE BEAUTIFUL COLORING PICTURES

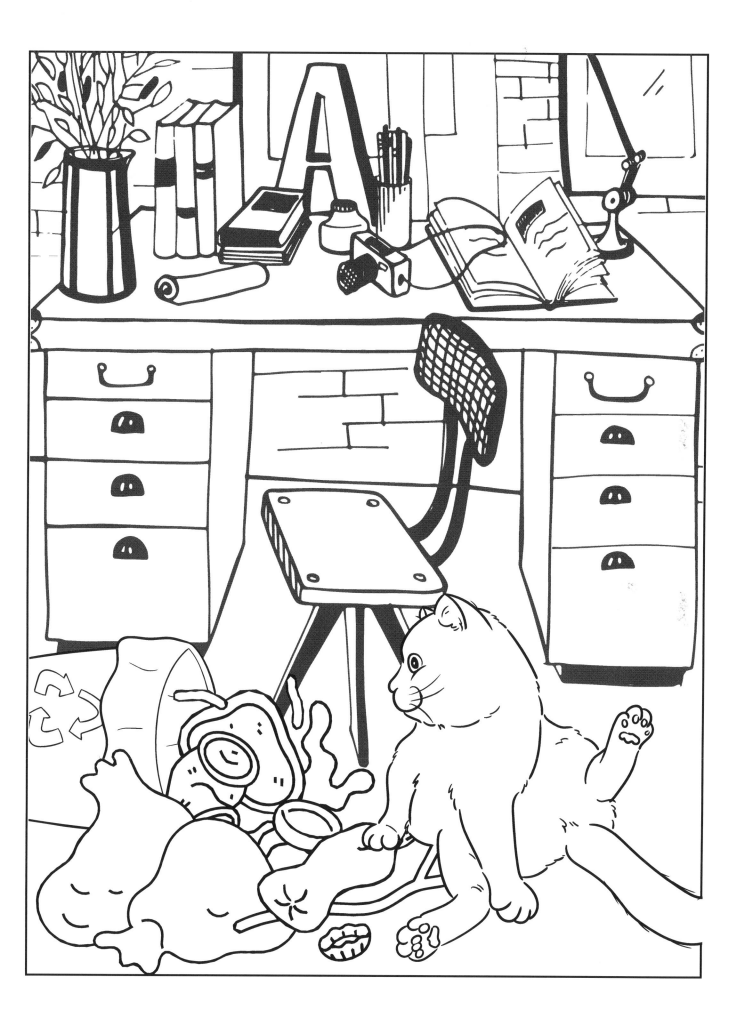

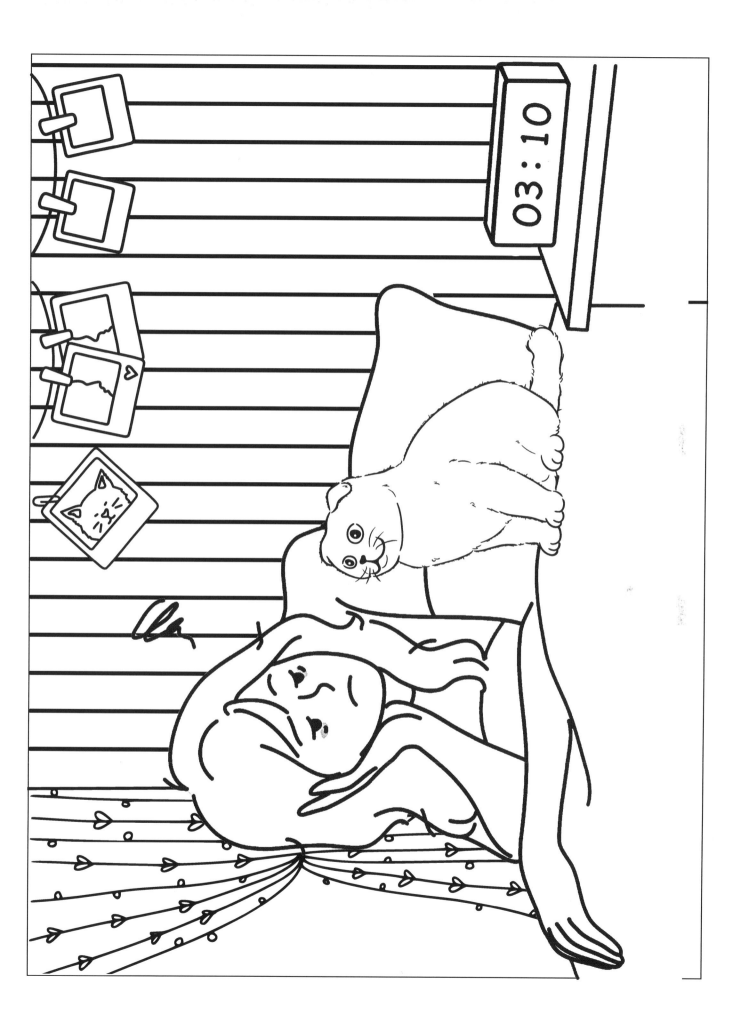

Made in the USA
Columbia, SC
07 December 2024

48669592R00046